MARTIAL ARTS for Kids

# A LOOK AT JUDO

Cara Krenn

Lerner Publications ◆ Minneapolis

Copyright © 2025 by Lerner Publishing Group, Inc.

All rights reserved. International copyright secured. No part of this book may be reproduced, stored in a retrieval system, or transmitted in any form or by any means—electronic, mechanical, photocopying, recording, or otherwise—without the prior written permission of Lerner Publishing Group, Inc., except for the inclusion of brief quotations in an acknowledged review.

Lerner Publications Company
An imprint of Lerner Publishing Group, Inc.
241 First Avenue North
Minneapolis, MN 55401 USA

For reading levels and more information, look up this title at www.lernerbooks.com.

Main body text set in Mikado.
Typeface provided by HVD.

**Editor:** Annie Zheng **Designer:** Mary Ross

**Library of Congress Cataloging-in-Publication Data**

Names: Krenn, Cara, author.
Title: A look at judo / Cara Krenn.
Description: Minneapolis, MN : Lerner Publications Company, [2025] | Series: Martial arts for kids (Lerner sports rookie) | Includes bibliographical references and index. | Audience: Ages 5–8 | Audience: Grades K–1 | Summary: "Judo is one of the world's most popular forms of martial arts! Young readers will enjoy learning more about the sport, how it works, how to compete, and more in this fun, high-interest book"— Provided by publisher.
Identifiers: LCCN 2024007744 (print) | LCCN 2024007745 (ebook) | ISBN 9798765647967 (library binding) | ISBN 9798765656198 (epub)
Subjects: LCSH: Judo—Juvenile literature.
Classification: LCC GV1114 .K74 2025 (print) | LCC GV1114 (ebook) | DDC 796.815/2—dc23/eng/20240222

LC record available at https://lccn.loc.gov/2024007744
LC ebook record available at https://lccn.loc.gov/2024007745

ISBN 979-8-7656-6207-6 (pbk)

Manufactured in the United States of America
1-1011021-53357-5/13/2024

# Table of Contents

| | | |
|---|---|---|
| Chapter 1 | What Is Judo? | 4 |
| Chapter 2 | Judo Basics | 10 |
| Chapter 3 | What to Expect | 16 |
| Chapter 4 | Judo Champ | 20 |

| | |
|---|---|
| Glossary | 24 |
| Learn More | 24 |
| Index | 24 |

CHAPTER 1

# What Is Judo?

One player holds another in a strong hold. They prepare to throw. It's time for judo!

Judo is a martial art. Martial arts are self-defense skills that people practice for sport.

**FUN FACT**

Judo started in Japan. People practice it all over the world.

Judo players are fast and strong. They throw an opponent to the ground. They use their bodies to pin another person down.

# CHAPTER 2
# Judo Basics

Judo students wear a cloth jacket and pants. They close their jacket with a belt. Players are barefoot.

**FUN FACT**

Beginners wear white belts. Black belts are for experts.

Judo takes place on a mat. In lessons, students learn how to fall safely. They dive and roll. Students practice drills over and over.

A judo fight is called a match. Matches are short. They are just a few minutes long.

CHAPTER 3

# What to Expect

In judo, players cannot punch or kick. They grip their opponent's jacket. They earn points when they make someone fall.

Judo players respect their teachers and other players. They stay calm on the mat.

# UP CLOSE!
## Judo Scoring

The highest score in a judo match is called an ippon. There are many ways to earn an ippon. One way is by throwing an opponent on their back. An ippon wins the match!

# CHAPTER 4
# Judo Champ

Students compete against players of the same size and strength. Players start and end a match with a bow.

**FUN FACT**

Judo is an Olympic sport.

Judo is hard work. But it can be lots of fun! Are you ready to start?

## Glossary

**drill:** exercise routine

**grip:** to hold tightly

**opponent:** a player you compete against

## Learn More

Catarevas, Eve Nadel. *Rena Glickman, Queen of Judo*. Minneapolis: Kar-Ben, 2022.
Coupé, Jessica. *Judo*. New York: Lightbox Learning, 2022.
Roza, Greg. *Judo*. New York: PowerKids, 2020.

## Index

belt, 10–11

hold, 4

match, 14, 19–20

pin, 8

throw, 4, 8, 19

## Photo Acknowledgments

Image credits: lechatnoir/Getty Images, pp. 5, 7, 13, 23; Oksana Shufrych/Getty Images, p. 9; fotokostic/Getty Images, p. 11; AP Photo/Abaca Press, p. 15; roibu/Shutterstock, p. 17; Victor Velter/Shutterstock, p. 18; David Finch/Getty Images, p. 19; AP Photo/Koji Ito, p. 21. Design elements: str33tcat/Getty Images; ulimi/Getty Images; Tuomas A. Lehtinen/Getty Images. Cover: CasarsaGuru/Getty Images.